DATE DUE			

Backyard Animals
Coyotes

Christine Webster

Weigl Publishers Inc.

Published by Weigl Publishers Inc.
350 5th Avenue, Suite 3304, PMB 6G
New York, NY 10118-0069
Website: www.weigl.com

Library of Congress Cataloging-in-Publication Data

Webster, Christine.
  Coyotes / Christine Webster.
     p. cm. -- (Backyard animals)
  ISBN 978-1-59036-673-8 (hard cover : alk. paper) -- ISBN 978-1-59036-674-5 (soft
cover : alk. paper)
  1. Coyote--Juvenile literature. I. Title.
  QL737.C22W43 2008
  599.77'25--dc22

                          2006102036

Printed in the United States of America
1 2 3 4 5 6 7 8 9 0 11 10 09 08 07

Editor Heather C. Hudak
Design and Layout Terry Paulhus

Cover: Coyotes live across North and Central America.

Contents

Meet the Coyote

Sometimes at night, animals can be heard howling in the distance. These are likely coyotes. Coyotes look similar to **domestic** dogs. A coyote is about the size of a German shepherd dog. Coyotes are leaner. They often look underfed even when healthy. They weigh about 20 to 50 pounds (9 to 23 kilograms).

Coyotes can be gray, brown, or tan in color. They have a bushy tail, pointed ears, and a narrow **muzzle**. Coyotes have green or yellowish eyes.

Coyotes live all over North America. They **adapt** easily to their surroundings. Coyotes thrive around farms and towns. Here, it is easy for coyotes to find food, such as garbage, small animals, and bird seed.

Fascinating Facts

Coyotes do not live where there are wolves. Both animals compete to eat many of the same foods, such as small animals.

Coyotes live in forests, deserts, mountains, and cities.

All about Coyotes

Coyotes belong to the dog **family**. The dog family has many **species**, such as wolves, foxes, jackals, and coyotes.

Members of the dog family share common features. They all give birth to live young. The structure of their teeth is similar. As well, each animal in the dog family walks on its toes instead of the soles of its feet.

Members of the dog family communicate by barking. They whimper, growl, and howl. Coyotes can make 11 different sounds.

A coyote's howl can be heard up to 3 miles (4.8 km) away.

Dog Family Facts

Bush Dog
- Lives in Central and South America
- Feet are partially webbed

Dhole
- Is found in eastern Asia
- Known for making a whistling sound

Domestic Dog
- Most common animal for a family pet
- Domesticated from wolves about 100,000 years ago

Gray Wolf
- Weighs between 55 and 115 pounds (25 and 52 kg)
- Largest species in the dog family

Golden Jackal
- Lives in Asia, Europe, and Africa
- Weighs between 15 and 30 pounds (7 and 14 kg)

Red Fox
- Lives in North America, Europe, Asia, North Africa, and Australia
- Weighs 6 to 15 pounds (2.7 to 6.8 kg)

Coyote History

Coyotes have been on Earth for a long time. There is proof that dog-like animals lived 55 to 38 million years ago. These animals may have been related to coyotes.

In 1823, an explorer named Thomas Say was the first person to publish a description of coyotes. He named the animals *Canis latrans*. This means "barking dog."

At first, coyotes lived in the prairie and desert regions of North America. As settlers moved across the country, they killed many wolves. Wolves were a **predator** of the coyote. Without wolves, coyotes could move safely from place to place. Today, coyotes live all over North America.

Fascinating Facts

Coyotes choose dens in hidden places. This helps them protect their pups, or babies, from predators.

The term "coyote" is Spanish. It comes from the Aztec word *coyotl*.

Coyote Shelter

Coyotes bed in places that are sheltered from poor weather. A female builds a den when she is raising pups. A den is a tunnel with a wide opening. The tunnel is about 5 to 30 feet (1.5 to 9 meters) long. It is about 3 feet (0.9 m) underground.

Female coyotes dig dens with their forepaws. They may make a second entrance to use if the other is blocked. Often, coyotes pile dirt against the den's entrance to keep out predators.

Dens can be found at the base of a hollow tree, between rocks, or on a steep hill. Sometimes, a coyote will take over the abandoned, or empty, home of a badger. Coyotes may use the same den for many years. If the den is disturbed, a coyote will find a new place to live.

Coyotes may have more than one den. If predators come nearby, coyotes will move to another den.

Coyotes are deep sleepers. They sleep so soundly that other animals can approach without being noticed.

Coyote Features

A coyotes' body has many special features to help it survive in nature. Coyotes have a keen sense of hearing and thick, warm fur. Most coyotes stand about 24 to 30 inches (61 to 76 centimeters) high at the shoulder. Often, females are smaller than males. No matter the size, each coyote has similar body parts.

EARS
Coyotes have wide, pointed ears that stand up on the top of their head. They have excellent hearing. This helps them hunt and avoid predators.

EYES
Coyotes have yellowish or green eyes with black pupils. Their eyes slant slightly. Coyotes' sharp eyesight helps them locate and catch **prey**.

TEETH
A coyote has long, pointed canine teeth. These front teeth are about 1.5 inches (3.8 cm) in length. Coyotes use their teeth to catch and eat their prey.

FUR

A coyote's soft fur is gray, tan, or brown. Often the fur on the coyote's back is black-tipped. Its long fur helps to protect the animal from the cold. The fur turns dark in the summer and light in the winter. This allows coyotes to blend in with their surroundings.

LEGS

A coyote's legs are strong and can move at speeds ranging from 25 to 40 miles (40 to 64 km) per hour. Coyotes use their legs to swim.

PAWS

A coyote has four paws, each with four, clawed toes. Coyotes have a fifth toe on their front feet. This is called the dewclaw. The coyote's front paws are larger than its back paws.

What Do Coyotes Eat?

Coyotes are omnivores. They eat both meat and plants. Their main diet is made up of mice, small rabbits, birds, large insects, grasshoppers, and rodents. Coyotes eat nuts and berries, too.

Much of a coyote's night is spent hunting for food. Coyotes hunt animals in many ways. When hunting smaller animals, coyotes often hunt alone. They slowly **stalk** their prey before suddenly pouncing on the animal.

If coyotes want to catch a larger animal, such as a deer or a sheep, they may hunt in groups. The coyotes each take turns chasing the animal until it tires.

Coyotes will watch the sky for circling birds. Birds often circle the sky above food sources.

Coyotes cover about 2.5 miles (4 km) of land as they hunt each night.

Coyote Life Cycle

Coyotes live in family groups. They mate for life. This means that they remain with the same partner until one of them dies.

Coyotes mate in February or March. About two months later, the babies are born.

Pups

A coyote pup is covered with brown fur at birth. It cannot see, and its eyes remain closed for eight to ten days. Coyote pups drink their mother's milk for two to six weeks. Both male and female coyotes care for their young. The pups do not leave the den for the first few weeks.

3 Weeks to 1 Year Old

At about three weeks of age, pups will romp around under their parents' watchful eyes. Later, the adults teach the pups to hunt. By autumn, the pups weigh about 20 pounds (9 kg). They are old enough to find their own food and leave their parents' den.

Most females have about three to seven pups at a time. They can have up to 12 pups in one **litter**. In nature, coyotes live between 8 and 10 years.

Adult

A coyote is considered an adult when it reaches one year of age. Some may leave their parents around this time. However, they often stay to form a pack. A pack can have two parents, young pups, and a new litter. Sometimes, the newly adult coyotes will help their parents feed the new litter. They will hunt and gather food.

Encountering Coyotes

Coyotes should not be approached. If a person encounters a coyote in nature, he or she should not run away. It is important to leave calmly and make loud noises to scare the coyote away. People should never try to touch, feed, or tame a coyote.

Coyotes sometimes roam cities and towns where people live. They may hunt small animals, such as cats and dogs, that live here. The smell of garbage may bring coyotes to cities. It is important to keep garbage tightly sealed and small animals indoors. Small children should be watched while outdoors.

Useful Websites

To learn more about what to do when encountering coyotes, check out
**www.wcsv.org/Education/
Coyote_Solutions.htm**

Bears, mountain lions, and wolves were once the coyote's main predators. Today, humans are the coyote's major threat.

Myths and Legends

Many American Indian stories describe how clever coyotes are. They also portray the coyote as a trickster. Some American Indians believed that the coyote has special powers. They thought that it could **transform** beings and objects. They believed that a coyote could make important decisions as well. The Navajo people often dressed in coyote skins during ceremonies.

One story talks about a cowboy named Pecos Bill. Pecos Bill fell out of a covered wagon as a baby. Coyotes raised him as one of their own. Pecos Bill thought he was a coyote until he was 18 years old.

The Aztec people believed the feathered coyote was the companion of Tezcatlipoca. This was the Lord of Night and of Wars.

Coyote and Salmon

Here is a version of a legend passed down by the Secwepemc Peoples.

Coyote wanted to give a feast to the people, so he caught and dried some salmon. He even made salmon oil and buried salmon eggs. Then, he sent out messengers to invite everyone. He decided he would sing and dance for the people. He thought to himself, "They will think I am a great man."

Coyote practiced. He danced in and out between the poles of drying fish. Suddenly, his hair became caught in a salmon gill. Coyote pulled the fish off and threw it in the river. All the salmon then came to life. They jumped off the poles and ran into the river.

Coyote tried to catch them but could not. As he reached for the last salmon, the salmon oil sprang to life. It ran to the river. Even the salmon eggs he had buried jumped back into the river. When the people came, there was no salmon. They thought Coyote had played a trick on them.

Frequently Asked Questions

Why are coyotes becoming more common in cities and towns?

Answer: Coyotes are less afraid of humans. They know that they can quickly and easily find food near people.

When are coyotes most active?

Answer: Coyotes are nocturnal. This means they are most active at night. They also are active at dusk and dawn.

What is the difference between the track of a domestic dog and a coyote track?

Answer: In a track, the slender back pad of a coyote is often not as visible as that of a dog's pad. A coyote's tracks often are longer than a dog's tracks.

Puzzler

See if you can answer these questions about coyotes.

1. How many sounds can a coyote use to communicate?
2. Do coyotes mate for life?
3. What do coyotes eat?
4. Name four other species in the dog family.
5. When do coyotes hunt?

Answers: 1. 11 2. yes 3. mice, small rabbits, birds, large insects, grasshoppers, rodents, nuts, and berries 4. gray wolf, red fox, golden jackal, domestic dog, dhole, bush dog 5. at night

Find Out More

There are many more interesting facts to learn about coyotes. If you would like to learn more, look for these books at your library.

Perry, Phyllis J. *Crafty Canines: Coyotes, Foxes and Wolves.* Franklin Watts, 2000.

Swanson, Diane. *Welcome to the World of Coyotes.* Walrus Books, 2002.

Words to Know

adapt: to adjust to the natural environment

domestic: an animal that has been trained to live with people

family: a group of related animals

litter: many babies born at one time to the same mother

muzzle: the nose, mouth, and jaw of an animal

predator: an animal that hunts other animals for food

prey: an animal that is hunted by another animal for food

species: animals or plants that share certain features

stalk: to follow another animal quietly in order to catch it

transform: to change in form, look, or shape

Index